THE FACTS ON
JEHOVAH'S WITNESSES

John Ankerberg
& John Weldon

Verses marked NIV are taken from the Holy Bible, New International Version, Copyright © 1973, 1978, 1984 by the International Bible Society. Used by permission of Zondervan Bible Publishers.

Verses marked NASB are taken from the New American Standard Bible, © 1960, 1962, 1963, 1968, 1971, 1972, 1973, 1975, 1977 by The Lockman Foundation. Used by permission.

Verses marked NWT are taken from the New World Translation © the Watchtower Bible and Tract Society, Brooklyn, NY.

THE FACTS ON JEHOVAH'S WITNESSES

Copyright © 1988 by Harvest House Publishers
Eugene, Oregon 97402

ISBN 0-89081-733-2

Printed in the United States of America.

CONTENTS

SECTION I—Introduction

SECTION II—The Worldview
of the Jehovah's Witnesses: Practices and Teachings

SECTION III—The Theology of
the Jehovah's Witnesses

SECTION IV—Analysis and Critique:
Does God Speak Only Through the Watchtower Society?

FOUR TESTS EXAMINING THIS CLAIM

*Test One: If God Speaks Only Through The Watchtower
Society, Then The New World Translation (or* NWT) *Must Be
Accurate—But Is It?*

Other books by John Ankerberg and John Weldon

The Facts on Astrology
The Facts on False Teaching in the Church
The Facts on the New Age Movement
The Facts on Spirit Guides
The Facts on Angels

SECTION I
Introduction

1. Who are the Jehovah's Witnesses?

The Jehovah's Witnesses are a religious sect begun by
Charles Taze Russell in the 1870s. In formulating their
beliefs, Russell drew on the teachings of such sects as Sev-
enth-Day Adventism and Christadelphianism, plus his own
interpretation of the Bible.[1] Through aggressive, door-to-
door proselytizing and authoritarian leadership, the group
has grown from a small number of Bible students to about
2.5 million members in over 200 countries and territories.*

2. Who are the leaders of the Jehovah's Witnesses?

The leaders of the Jehovah's Witnesses are a group of
men who head an organization called the Watchtower Bible
and Tract Society, or simply the Watchtower Society, in
Brooklyn, New York. This small group wields absolute spiritual authority over the 2.5 million members. The Society is
headed by a president who rules for life. To date, it has had
four presidents, each of whom has left his unique mark on
the Society's religion.

3. How have the Watchtower Society's presidents shaped the organization?

Each president has governed with absolute power. As a
result, his period of rule has been marked by his unique
personality and Bible interpretation. Thus there have been
four distinct "periods" of the Society: 1) the period of Charles
Taze Russell (1872-1916); 2) the period of "Judge" Joseph F.
Rutherford (1917-1942); 3) the period of Nathan H. Knorr
(1942-1977); 4) the period of Frederick W. Franz (1977-
present).

---

*The Jehovah's Witnesses claim 3.2 million members in over 200 coun-
tries and territories (see the *1987 Yearbook of The Jehovah's Witnesses*,
pp. 2, 254) although this figure may not take into account a large
number of defections and disfellowshippings.

Because the Witnesses claim that God Himself was and is the source or author of their Bible interpretations and doctrines, it is important to examine these four periods. Doing so reveals the surprising fact that each president has interpreted the Bible *differently* from or even in *contradiction* of the others. Examining the writings of these men plainly shows that the claim of the Jehovah's Witnesses that God is the author of all of the Society's doctrines is absurd. The Bible teaches that God is not the author of confusion (1 Corinthians 14:33). The Society, then, is guided not by God, but by fallible men.

Charles Taze Russell, the Society's founder, wrote a new "Bible" for the faithful of his day, which he claimed "came from God through the enlightenment of the Holy Spirit."[2] This was the seven-volume *Studies in the Scriptures.** He taught that this material was necessary for properly understanding the Bible. In their principal publication, *The Watchtower* magazine, Sept. 15, 1910, p. 298, Russell wrote that without *Studies in the Scriptures* one could never "see the divine plan in studying the Bible by itself." Further, he said, even after reading *Studies in the Scriptures* for ten years, if one stopped reading it and went to "the Bible alone," "within two years he [would revert back] into darkness." Conversely, one who never read the Bible but did read Russell's volumes "would be in the light at the end of two years because he would have had the light of the Scriptures."[3] In other words, Russell claimed that a new divine interpreter was needed to understand the Bible properly. And he claimed to be that interpreter.

Yet today the Watchtower Society contradicts many of Russell's doctrines and "divine interpretations" of Scripture. The true "divine interpreter" has changed. It is now no longer Russell but the Society itself. It claims the same authority Russell did: that only its interpretations of the Bible are authoritative, and that studying the Bible alone will lead to darkness and heresy.

For example, *The Watchtower*, Aug. 15, 1981, condemns those who:

> say that it is sufficient to read the Bible exclusively, either alone or in small groups at home.
> ...Through such "Bible reading," they have

---

*Technically, Vol. 7, *The Finished Mystery,* was posthumously compiled and edited by George H. Fisher and Clayton J. Woodworth.

> reverted right back to the apostate doctrines
> that commentaries by Christendom's clergy
> were teaching 100 years ago. . . .[4]

It is interesting that the Watchtower Society itself admits that anyone who reads the Bible alone will come to the same beliefs that orthodox Christianity has always held. Nevertheless, the writings Russell once called indispensable for understanding the Bible (his own) are today largely ignored.

Under the direction of the second president, "Judge" Rutherford, the organization became even more authoritarian. Rutherford instituted an "era of changes" and ignored, altered, or denied hundreds or thousands of Russell's teachings. He justified these changes by claiming a "progressive revelation" that permitted him to shed "new light" on Russell's ideas.[5]

This is why thousands of faithful followers of Russell, realizing Rutherford had abandoned Russell, left the organization. They believed Russell's claim that he was inspired by God and felt that to change his teachings drastically was to deny God. The broad majority of Witnesses, however, accepted the changes without question.

During the third major era, under the organizational leadership of Nathan H. Knorr, the number of Witnesses grew from 105,000 to about 2.2 million. New stress was placed on training in the Jehovah's Witnesses' interpretations of the Bible. A new Bible translation was produced to support these interpretations—and additional changes in Bible interpretation and doctrine occurred.[6]

The current era, under President Frederick W. Franz, could be labeled an "era of crisis" because thousands of Witnesses have begun to examine the history of the Society independently. They have become convinced that it is not God's organization and have left it or been disfellowshipped.

Even President Fredrick W. Franz's nephew, Raymond, is an example of one who has left the Watchtower. His book *Crisis of Conscience* shows why the Watchtower Society cannot be "God's sole channel" on earth. His text is an authoritative exposé by a key leader familiar with the inner workings of the Society. It portrays an authoritarian group of men who go to great lengths to retain their image of divine guidance. Raymond Franz concludes that the Society is not of God. He cites evidence that it 1) is antibiblical, 2) has given extensive false prophecies, 3) has changed its teachings and policies, 4) has engaged in lying and cover-ups, and 5) has brought destruction into the lives of some of its members.[7] "Most of the [Governing] Body were actually not that well versed in the Scriptures," he writes (p. 97). They practiced "manipulation of Scripture and fact" to uphold their interpretations of the Bible (p. 245). The emphasis was "not loyalty to God and His Word, but loyalty to the organization and its teachings" (p. 257). The Society has reacted to those who question its authority with the threat of disfellowshipping. For most Jehovah's Witnesses, disfellowshipping means not only losing friends but also being separated or cut off from family.

4. What attracts people to the Jehovah's Witnesses?

Many people are attracted to the Jehovah's Witnesses because they claim to have authoritative answers to many of life's problems. In a society torn by relative values and personal insecurities, any group is attractive that 1) claims to offer divine guidance; 2) claims to provide genuine solutions to life's problems; and 3) stresses moral and family values. The Watchtower Society is appealing to people who are looking for answers, who are frightened about the future, or who are tired of the lack of moral values in America. They are drawn to the dedication and commitment that the Witnesses show.

In addition, many people in mainline churches who have never been taught the Bible by their pastors desire to know it better. They are grateful to Witnesses who devote a lot of time and effort to allegedly helping them understand the Bible better.

SECTION II

The Worldview of the Jehovah's Witnesses: Practices and Teachings

5. What is the religious worldview of the Jehovah's Witnesses, and what logical results flow from it?

Three basic beliefs, or assumptions, form the religious worldview of the Jehovah's Witnesses:

a) *Divine guidance comes only through the Watchtower Society.* This assumption leads Witnesses to live under an authoritarian organization that suppresses independent thinking in the name of God. Once a member accepts the organization's policies and decisions as being God's will, disagreement with the Watchtower Society is disagreement with God. It follows then that any criticism of the Society is defined as satanic. The Society teaches that "Jehovah's organization is in no wise [way] democratic. ... His government or organization is strictly theocratic" (which means ruled by God alone).[8]

b) *Jehovah's Witnesses alone have the truth of God. They alone are the people of God.* This follows logically from their first assumption that divine guidance comes only from the Watchtower. This belief causes an attitude of exclusivism that stresses their uniqueness and superiority. This, in turn, leads them to accept an alleged divine command to be separate from the entire world system—social, political, military, and religious. Witnesses view the whole world system as satanic.

The Watchtower tells them with divine authority that Jehovah's Witnesses are to be separate and renounce such things as military service, patriotism, and celebrating religious holidays (see Question 7). Children of Jehovah's Witnesses are not permitted to engage in school activities prohibited by the Society—like Christmas plays, saluting the flag, and the Pledge of Allegiance—which results in their having considerably more difficulty growing up than do most other children.

c) *Jehovah's Witnesses are told that Orthodox, Protestant, and Catholic Christianity are false and controlled by Satan.* Because of this belief, Witnesses avoid all other Christians and completely reject their idea of the Christian faith (see Question 8).

8

6. Does the Watchtower Society really claim to be the only organization on earth through which God works?

The Watchtower Society does claim that of all religious organizations, God works only through it. It alone has authority to speak for God.[9] For example, *The Watchtower* states:

> We belong to NO earthly organization. ...We adhere only to that heavenly organization.... All the saints now living or that ever lived during this age, belong to OUR CHURCH ORGANIZATION: such are all ONE CHURCH, and there is NO OTHER recognized by the Lord.[10]

Thus, Jehovah's Witnesses believe that no one on earth can discover the complete will of God apart from the Watchtower Society. Only the Watchtower Society and its publications can reveal the true meaning of the Bible. The Society is seen as "God's sole collective channel for the flow of biblical truth to men on earth."[11]

One Jehovah's Witness said to a Christian, "Your Bible was finished 2000 years ago, but our Bible has 32 pages added to it every week." He was referring to *The Watchtower*, a magazine that Witnesses are taught is the Word of God.[12]

A former member wrote,

> We were taught that we must adhere absolutely to the decisions and scriptural understandings of the Society, because God had given it this authority over His people (*The Watchtower*, May 10, 1972, p. 272).... To gain...eternal life, I was told certain things were necessary: (1) I should study the Bible diligently, and only through Watchtower publications....[13]

The Watchtower of Feb. 15, 1983, p. 12, stated as a requirement of salvation "...that we be associated with God's channel, His organization.... To receive everlasting life in the earthly paradise we must identify that organization and serve God as part of it."

Thus, from the above statements, it is clear that the Watchtower Society claims to be the only organization on earth through which God works.

7. Why do Jehovah's Witnesses prohibit practices like military service, saluting the flag, celebrating holidays, and blood transfusions?

These and many other practices are prohibited because the entire world system, apart from activity in the Watchtower Organization, is believed to be connected with the devil. Military service, patriotism, and celebrating holidays are all part of the devil's scheme to trick men away from God. Thus the Society asks, "Do you want to be part of Satan's world or are you for God's new system? ... getting out of Babylon the Great, the world empire of false religion ... also means having nothing to do with the religious celebrations of the world."[14]

Other practices are prohibited because they are wrongly thought to be prohibited by Scripture. Although the Bible only forbids *eating* blood (something associated with pagan rituals), the Society has wrongly interpreted this as a ban on blood *transfusions*, something entirely different. The Witnesses teach that accepting a blood transfusion may "cost ... [one his] eternal life...."[15] Tragically, hundreds, perhaps even thousands of Witnesses and their children, have died because they have believed the Watchtower's unbiblical view.[15a]

8. What do Jehovah's Witnesses believe about Christianity?

The Jehovah's Witnesses believe that Christianity is an apostate religion that has taught false doctrines and deceived people for over 1800 years. Until Jehovah's Witnesses appeared in the late nineteenth century and began teaching the Bible correctly, God's truth was largely absent from the world. Thus, the Witnesses believe that the Christian Church is a satanic deception and that they alone are the true church.

Consider the following statements that have been made by some of the Watchtower presidents and official leaders:

- "Jehovah's Christian Witnesses are the ones that have identified who Babylon the Great is ... the world empire of false religion. The chief component member and mouthpiece in that religious world empire is Christendom! She is the most reprehensible member thereof because she claims to be 'Christian.' Her blasphemies exceed those of 'pagandom.' ... Her blood guilt exceeds that of all the non-Christian religious realm."[16]

- "Christendom's course is 'the way of death.'..."[17]
- "The Anglo-American empire system, which chiefly is 'Christendom,' Satan makes his chief spokesman on earth...."[18]
- "Christendom's religion is demonism...."[19]
- "As the most reprehensible ones among the people of Christendom, the clergy and religious leaders will drink the potion of death...."[20]

It is clear from this that Jehovah's Witnesses view Christians and the Christian faith as one of their most powerful and hated enemies. Does this mean they have compassion on Christians and hope to rescue them from their collision course with God's judgment? Do they take Jesus seriously and love their enemies (Matthew 5:44)? Far from it! They are taught:

> Haters of God and His people...are to be hated....We must hate in the truest sense, which is to regard with extreme and active aversion, to consider as loathsome, odious, filthy, to detest. Surely any haters of God are not fit to live on this beautiful earth....We must have a proper perspective of these enemies....We cannot love those hateful enemies, for they are fit only for destruction....We pray with intensity...and plead that [Jehovah's] anger be made manifest....Oh, Jehovah God of Hosts ...be not merciful to any wicked transgressors ...consume them in wrath, consume them that they shall be no more.[21]

Jehovah's Witnesses believe what the Watchtower has taught them even though Jesus plainly says in their own Bible they are to "continue to love your enemies...that you may prove yourselves sons of your father who is in the heavens" (Matthew 5:44-45, NWT).

SECTION III

The Theology of the Jehovah's Witnesses

9. What do Jehovah's Witnesses believe about God and the doctrine of the Trinity?

Jehovah's Witnesses believe that the God of Christianity is a false and satanic counterfeit of the one true God, Jehovah. Charles Taze Russell even wrote that the Christian God was "the devil himself."[22] Jehovah's Witnesses see God as a single person, not as a single Being in whom are united three Persons, as Christians view God. They also deny that God is present everywhere and limit His omniscience.[23]

Because the Watchtower Society teaches that God is only one person, Witnesses reject the doctrine of the Trinity as an invention of "pagan imagination."[24] They call it "a false doctrine... promulgated [promoted] by Satan for the purposes of defaming Jehovah's name."[25]

The Watchtower Society often misrepresents the doctrine of the Trinity. But Christians do not teach the view of God that the Witnesses say they do. Christians do not teach there are "three Gods" or "a complicated, freakish-looking, three-headed God."[26]

Instead, Christians believe the Bible teaches that the one true God exists eternally as three Persons. The doctrine of the Trinity can be seen from five simple statements supported by the Bible. (Scriptures below taken from the Jehovah's Witnesses' *New World Translation*, 1970 ed., are abbreviated NWT.[27])

1. *There is only one true God*: "For there is one God, and one mediator between God and men...." (1 Timothy 2:5, NWT; cf. Deuteronomy 4:35; 6:4; Isaiah 43:10)

2) *The Father is God*: "There is actually to us one God the Father.... (1 Corinthians 8:6, NWT; cf. John 17:1-3; 2 Corinthians 1:3; Philippians 2:11; Colossians 1:3; 1 Peter 1:2)

3) *Jesus Christ, the Son, is God*: "...but he [Jesus] was also calling God his own Father, making himself equal to God." (John 5:18, NWT); "In answer Thomas said to him [Jesus]: 'My Lord and my God!'" (John 20:28, NWT; cf. Isaiah 9:6; John 1:1; Romans 9:5; Titus 2:13; 2 Peter 1:1—see note 27.)

4) *The Holy Spirit* is a *Person,* is *eternal,* and is *therefore God.* The Holy Spirit is a *Person:* "However, when that one arrives, the spirit of the truth, *he* will guide you into all the truth, for *he* will not speak of *his* own impulse, but what things *he* hears *he* will speak, and *he* will declare to you the things coming." (John 14:13, NWT, emphasis added) The Holy Spirit is *eternal:* "How much more will the blood of the Christ, who through an everlasting spirit offered himself without blemish to God...." (Hebrews 9:14, NWT) The Holy Spirit is *therefore God:* "But Peter said: 'Ananias, why has Satan emboldened you to play false to the holy spirit.... You have played false, not to men, but to God.'" (Acts 5:3,4, NWT)

5) *The Father, Son and Holy Spirit are distinct Persons:* "...Baptizing them in the name of the Father and of the Son and of the holy spirit"; "The undeserved kindness of the Lord Jesus Christ and the love of God and the sharing in the holy spirit be with all of you." (Matthew 28:19; 2 Corinthians 13:14, NWT).

It is clear from these verses read either from the *New World Translation* (NWT) or a modern version like the *New International Version* (NIV) that the Bible teaches the one true God exists eternally as Father, Son, and Holy Spirit. For 1900 years the historic Christian church has found in the Bible the doctrine of the Trinity as defined above. This can be seen by anyone who reads the Church Fathers and studies the historic Creeds.[28]

Man's incomplete comprehension of this truth is no reason to reject what Scripture teaches, as the Watchtower Society itself agrees:

> Sincere seekers for the truth want to know what is right. They realize they would only be fooling themselves if they rejected portions of God's Word while claiming to base their beliefs on other parts.[29]

Nevertheless, Jehovah's Witnesses allow human reason to judge God's Word. They reject the Bible's teaching about the one true God existing as three Persons and replace it in favor of their own view that God is only one Person. Because the idea of a triune God is to them "unreasonable," they think that it cannot be true.[30]

To see how unreasonable the Witnesses are in thinking this way, let's consider a scientific illustration.

Scientists long believed that all energy existed as either "waves" or "particles": two contradictory things. They felt it could not possibly be both because their natures were different. But modern scientific tests surprised scientists and indicated to them that light existed as both waves *and* particles. For a while some couldn't accept this conclusion because it wasn't reasonable. So some scientists insisted that light was only waves, while others insisted that it was only particles. Finally, though, scientists were forced by the *evidence* to conclude that light really was both waves and particles. Rather than clinging doggedly to their preconceived notions of reality, the evidence forced them to accept a different conclusion.

There is no scientist who understands this fact or who can explain it reasonably. But they are honest enough to accept this is what light is.

In the same way, God has told us who He is. The evidence of Scripture forces us to accept that the one true God exists as Father, Son, and Holy Spirit. We may not be able to understand it or explain it reasonably, but we accept it because this is what the facts have led us to.

Another illustration is love. Hardly anyone really *understands* what love is, how it works, how it begins, how it grows, or anything else connected with it. Yet we don't question its reality merely because we can't fully understand it.

Jehovah's Witnesses don't deny the reality of light or love merely because they don't fully understand them. Why then, do they insist that they must understand God before they accept His existence as He has revealed it?

Indeed, Father, Son, and Holy Spirit are so effortlessly and consistently linked in Scripture that assuming that God is not three Persons makes it impossible to understand some passages (e.g., Matthew 28:19; 2 Corinthians 1:21,22; 13:14; Ephesians 2:18; 3:11-16; 5:18-20; 1 Thessalonians 1:1-5).

Try answering the following questions without concluding that the Bible teaches the doctrine of the Trinity:

1) Who raised Jesus from the dead? The Father (Romans 6:4; Acts 3:26; 1 Thessalonians 1:10)? The Son (John 2:19-21; 10:17,18)? The Holy Spirit (Romans 8:11)? Or God (Hebrews 13:20; Acts 13:30; 17:31)?

2) Who does the Bible say is God? The Father (Ephesians 4:6)? The Son (Titus 2:13; John 1:1; 20:28)? The Holy Spirit (Acts 5:3,4)? The one and only true God (Deuteronomy 4:35)?

3) Who created the world? The Father (John 14:2)? The Son (Colossians 1:16,17; John 1:1-3)? The Holy Spirit (Genesis 1:2; Psalm 104:30)? Or God (Genesis 1:1; Hebrews 11:3)?

4) Who saves man? Who *regenerates* man? The Father (1 Peter 1:3)? The Son (John 5:21; 4:14)? The Holy Spirit (John 3:6; Titus 3:5)? Or God (1 John 3:9)? Who *justifies* man? The Father (Jeremiah 23:6, cf. 2 Corinthians 5:19)? The Son (Romans 5:9; 10:4; 2 Corinthians 5:19,21)? The Holy Spirit (1 Corinthians 6:11; Galatians 5:5)? Or God (Romans 4:6; 9:33)? Who *sanctifies* man? The Father (Jude 1)? The Son (Titus 2:14)? The Holy Spirit (1 Peter 1:2)? Or God (Exodus 31:13)? Who *propitiated* God's just anger against man for his sins? The Father (1 John 4:14; John 3:16; 17:5; 18:11)? The Son (Matthew 26:28; John 1:29; 1 John 2:2)? The Holy Spirit (Hebrews 9:14)? Or God (2 Corinthians 5:1; Acts 20:28)?

Though Jehovah's Witnesses exalt human reason against the doctrine of the Trinity, saying that it is "unreasonable," people who submit their minds to God's Word must conclude that it is unreasonable *not* to believe in it.

10. What do Jehovah's Witnesses believe about Jesus?

The Jehovah's Witnesses teach that Jesus Christ was the first creation of God, the Archangel Michael.[31] They believe that He "had a beginning" and "was actually a creature of God."[32] By so believing, the Witnesses reject the Bible's teaching about Jesus.

But the Bible teaches that although Christ is fully man, He is also fully God (John 1:1; 5:18; 10:30; 20:28; Titus 2:13; Colossians 2:9; Philippians 2:1-8). It teaches that, as God, Christ is eternal, not created (Micah 5:2; John 1:1-3). All these verses the *New World Translation* dishonestly mistranslates (for examples, see Question 14).

The Witnesses wrongly teach that "Christ Jesus received immortality as a reward for his faithful course of action [on earth]...."[33] This is because "any failure on his part would have meant eternal death [extinction] for him."[34]

However, the Bible teaches something completely different. It teaches that, as God, Jesus was already immortal and could never have ceased to exist; He is the same yesterday, today, and forever (Hebrews 13:8). Neither did He have to earn His own salvation, since He was always sinless (Hebrews 4:15) and immortal (Isaiah 9:6) and needed no salvation.

According to the Witnesses, the fundamental identity of Jesus has been altered. They believe that the angel Michael was changed into the mortal man Jesus, thus ceasing to be an angel. Later the man Jesus was changed into an improved and immortal version of the angel Michael. This happened when God recreated the man Jesus after His death. The Jehovah's Witnesses deny the physical resurrection of Christ (John 2:19-21; 1 Corinthians 15:3,4,17,35-49), teaching instead that when God "recreated" Jesus He made Him an immortal angel. Jesus no longer existed and Michael had no access to Jesus' earthly body. As Russell wrote, "the man Jesus is dead, forever dead."[35]

But the Apostle Paul disagrees. Writing long after Jesus' death and resurrection, Paul taught that there "*is* one God and one mediator between God and men, the *man* Christ Jesus" (1 Timothy 2:5).

Thus, Jehovah's Witnesses deny the biblical teaching that Jesus is "the same yesterday and today and forever" (Hebrews 13:8).[36]

Finally, since the Witnesses teach that after Jesus' death, he was recreated a spirit creature (an angel), it is impossible that He could ever return to earth visibly and physically. Therefore, they teach that Michael returned invisibly in 1914.[37] But the Bible does not teach that Michael has or will return to earth. Rather, the Bible reveals that someday Jesus will return in a cataclysmic event and the entire world will recognize Him (Matthew 24:1-35). The Bible says Jesus will appear visibly, not invisibly, and physically, not spiritually, to all the world. The Bible says Jesus will appear in the same body He had while on earth, although now glorified (John 20:24-28; Acts 1:9-11; Zechariah 12:10).

The Christ of the Jehovah's Witnesses is not the Christ of the Bible.

11. What do Jehovah's Witnesses believe about salvation?

The Jehovah's Witnesses believe that there are three classes of people that will be saved by good works. But each class is working to gain a different salvation.

The *first* class is an extremely small group of people the Jehovah's Witnesses call "the 144,000." Only these are elected by God for special spiritual privileges. For example, many of the blessings that the Bible teaches are given to *every* believer by faith alone are, according to the Watchtower Society, reserved exclusively for the 144,000. For example, this class is said to enjoy the spiritual privileges and blessings of justification and being born again. However, justification and being born again are redefined. Justification is not a once-for-all legal declaration God makes about a believer, giving him a perfect and righteous standing before God on account of the atonement of Christ, as is taught in Scripture (Romans 3:28; Philippians 3:9). Rather, they say justification is a "present justification" that may be forfeited at any time by disobedience.[38]

They also redefine the words "born again." The Jehovah's Witnesses say that being born again is being water baptized and anointed by God so they may be recreated by God as a spirit creature after death, just as God supposedly recreated Jesus into the angel Michael after His death. (The Witnesses teach that Jesus was "born again" at His baptism.) According to the Witnesses, the 144,000 are spiritually privileged to eventually be recreated like Jesus, and also privileged to rule with Jesus in heaven.[39] They do not understand that the Bible really teaches that all men, not just the 144,000, can be born again. They do not realize that being born again is a spiritual rebirth in the inner man that God grants, which can occur during life and brings with it eternal life (John 3:3-8; 5:24; 6:47; 1 John 1:11-13, NWT).

The *second* class includes all other Jehovah's Witnesses (called "the other sheep"). They cannot be justified in this life or born again. Indeed, the average Jehovah's Witness has no hope of ever being born again. At death God does not recreate these people as spirit beings, as Jesus was changed into Michael, but recreates their physical bodies to live only on the earth. These people are told they will be ruled over by Jesus (Michael) and the 144,000 in heaven.

The *third* class includes non-Jehovah's Witnesses who have lived good enough lives to be given the opportunity to earn salvation after death (a teaching that the Bible denies—Hebrews 9:27). All who are worthy of the second chance will be recreated by Jehovah to live in the new millennium. But they will only gain life beyond the millennium if they attain perfection during it.[40]

Not one of the above teachings is biblical. The Bible says there is only one basis upon which God grants salvation, and it is offered freely to all men (Galatians 1:6-8; John 3:16; Acts 4:12). Again, the new birth and heavenly salvation are not limited to 144,000 people, but are given freely to every believer: "Believe on the Lord Jesus Christ and you will get saved... (Acts 16:31, NWT). Salvation is by grace through faith alone, not by any of our works of righteousness (Ephesians 2:8,9; Titus 3:5; Romans 3:28, NWT). In fact, because salvation is "by grace [God's unmerited favor], then it is no longer by works [by our works]; if it were, grace would no longer be grace" (Romans 11:6).

Jesus declares to *all* people, "You must be born again."
He warned that no one could be acceptable to God without a
spiritual rebirth in this life that comes through faith in Him
(John 3:3-18). He warns, "...unless you believe that I am He
[Here "He" applies to Himself—the divine name that God
called Himself in the Old Testament; cf. Exodus 3:14; Isaiah
43:10.], you shall die in your sins" (John 8:24).

*Salvation is by personal merit and good works, not by
grace through faith.*

For a Jehovah's Witness, "grace" is merely the opportunity for men to earn their own salvation. It is not the free
gift of God to men. Because Jehovah's Witnesses think they
must earn their own salvation, they have no concept of true
biblical grace.[41] Thus, the Society teaches that obeying
"God's commandments...can [might] mean an eternal
future,"[42] but this cannot give any *assurance* of salvation:

> ...in all areas of life, we should be prepared to
> give our very best. We should not be half-hearted
> about such vital matters. What is at stake is
> Jehovah's approval and our being granted life.[43]

The Bible, in stark contrast, teaches that no one by his own
good works can ever gain salvation (Romans 3:10-20, NWT).
The Bible says that salvation cannot be earned or maintained
by personal works of righteousness (Galatians 2:16,21, NWT).
It is available only to those who recognize that they are
unworthy and that they cannot earn it, who in repentance
turn from sin and place their faith in Christ's work at the
Cross for them (Romans 3:22; Luke 18:9-14, NWT).

But the Witnesses believe that God only justifies people
"on the basis of their own merit."[44] The Watchtower has lied to
them in teaching that salvation rests wholly on their good
works, obedience to God, and personal merit. If they back-
slide, their salvation is forfeited and they risk being annihilated forever.[45]

This means that the only "salvation" the Witness has is the
desperate hope that somehow as a fallen and sinful human
being he can, through his own efforts, finally win God's
approval. But only constant, diligent battling against sin
and total obedience to serving God through the Watchtower
gives him any hope of being recreated after death for millennial life. Even then, he is told that during the millennium if he fails he will be annihilated. If he serves faithfully
all through this 1000-year period of time, he may finally
win eternal life. But it will only be because he has earned it
by personal effort and merit.

But the good news for every Jehovah's Witness is that God's Word opposes the Watchtower's plan of salvation. In the Bible, God guarantees eternal life. The eternal life that God promises to give does not begin in a distant future but the very moment a person believes in Christ for forgiveness of sins. In proof of this, below we quote the Jehovah's Witnesses *New World Translation* (emphasis added).

"Most truly I say to you, He that hears my word and believes him that sent me *has* everlasting life, and he does not come into judgment but *has* passed over from death to life" (John 5:24, NWT).

"Most truly I say to you, He that believes *has* everlasting life" (John 6:47, NWT).

At the very moment a person accepts the work of Christ on his behalf and asks Jesus to save him, he is born again and made a new creation (John 3:1-16; 2 Corinthians 5:17). "For this is the will of my Father, that *everyone* [notice: this is not just the 144,000, but everyone] that beholds the Son and exercises faith in him should have everlasting life, and I will resurrect him at the last day" (John 6:40, NWT).

Even the *New World Translation* states salvation "is not owing to you, it is God's gift" (Ephesians 2:8,9, NWT). For a moment, let's think about what a gift is. If a boy brings a girl a box of candy or flowers and says, "This is a gift for you. All you have to do to get it is to go clean my house and wash my car." The girl would say, "If I clean your house and wash your car, then I would have earned it—it would no longer be a gift." A gift is something you get for nothing—when somebody pays for it and freely gives it. Girls know the difference between a loving gift and something you must earn. God says He is giving eternal life as a free gift. He can offer this gift because He sent Jesus to purchase it. The *New World Translation* says, "...but the *gift* God gives is everlasting life by Christ Jesus our Lord" (Romans 6:23, NWT, emphasis added). Further, the NWT emphatically states, "By this undeserved kindness, indeed, you *have been saved through faith*; and this *not* owing to you, it is God's *gift*. No, *it is not owing to works*, in order that no man should have grounds for boasting" (Ephesians 2:8,9, NWT, emphasis added.)

SECTION IV

Analysis and Critique: Does God Speak Only Through the Watchtower Society?

No question is more vital to the Jehovah's Witness than whether the Watchtower Society really is God's sole channel for communicating His will to mankind today. When we listen to the Society, are we listening to God? If we are, then we should listen carefully. But if we're not, then we should reject what it says.

There are four key tests by which we may discover whether or not the Watchtower Society is God's *only* channel for communicating His will to mankind today. If God does communicate to all of mankind through the Watchtower Society, then every test question below should be answered in a manner consistent with its claims.

TEST ONE: If God speaks only through the Watchtower Society, then the *New World Translation* must be accurate. But is it? (The next three questions examine their translation.)

---

12. *Do the Jehovah's Witnesses claim that their Bible (the* New World Translation, *or* NWT*) is accurate?*

The Watchtower claims that its translation of the Bible is highly accurate. It claims the *New World Translation* is the most accurate or one of the most accurate translations yet produced, and it states: "The translation must be appraised on its own merits."[46] (From these words the Jehovah's Witnesses clearly challenge outsiders to examine the accuracy of their translation.) In *All Scripture Is Inspired By God and Beneficial* it claims precise grammatical accuracy in translation and adds, "...the *New World Translation*... is accurate and reliable....a faithful translation of God's word."[47]

In the *New World Translation* itself, the Watchtower claims it has translated the Scriptures "as accurately as possible," with both a fear of and love for God—indeed with a great "sense of solemn responsibility."[48]

In *The Kingdom Interlinear Translation of the Greek Scriptures* it claims that its New Testament translation accurately renders "what the original language says and means" and that it does so unbiasedly, "without any sectarian religious coloration."[49]

The Watchtower Society has even gone so far as to say that God Himself has supervised its translation of the Bible by "angels of various ranks who controlled" the translators.

Current Society President F. W. Franz, along with then-president Nathan Knorr, headed the secret committee of seven translators. Franz testified in a court case in Edinborough, Scotland, Nov. 23, 1954. The *Scottish Daily Express* on Nov. 24, 1954, recorded his testimony word for word. In Franz' testimony he stated under oath: 1) that he and Knorr had the final word in translation; 2) that he (Franz) was head of the Society's publicity department; 3) that translations and interpretations came from God, invisibly communicated to the publicity department by "angels of various ranks who control[ed]" the translators.[50] These statements by the leaders and translators concerning the accuracy of their *New World Translation* is evidence that they are in agreement with the Watchtower's claim to be God's sole channel on earth.

13. What do recognized Greek scholars believe about the accuracy of the NWT?

Greek scholars, Christian and non-Christian, universally reject the NWT, calling it biased and inaccurate.

Until his recent death, Dr. Julius Mantey was one of the leading Greek scholars in the world. He was author of the *Hellenistic Greek Reader* and coauthor, with H. E. Dana, of *A Manual Grammar of the Greek New Testament*. Not only did he reject the NWT, he publicly demanded that the Society stop misquoting his *Grammar* to support it (see appendix). Of the NWT translation he wrote:

> I have never read any New Testament so badly translated as *The Kingdom Interlinear Translation of the Greek Scriptures*. In fact, it is not their translation at all. Rather, it is a distortion of the New Testament. The translators used what J. B. Rotherham had translated in 1893, in modern speech, and changed the readings in scores of passages to state what Jehovah's Witnesses believe and teach. That is *distortion*, not translation.[51]

Dr. Bruce Metzger, professor of New Testament language and literature at Princeton Theological Seminary and author of *The Text of the New Testament* (Oxford, 1968), observes, "The Jehovah's Witnesses have incorporated in their translations of the New Testament several quite erroneous renderings of the Greek."[52]

Dr. Robert Countess wrote his dissertation for his Ph.D. in Greek on the NWT. He concluded that the Jehovah's Witnesses' translation:

> ...has been sharply unsuccessful in keeping doctrinal considerations from influencing the actual translation....It must be viewed as a radically biased piece of work. At some points it is actually dishonest. At others it is neither modern nor scholarly. And interwoven throughout its fabric is inconsistent application of its own principles enunciated in the Foreword and Appendix.[53]

British scholar H. H. Rowley asserts, "From beginning to end this volume is a shining example of how the Bible should not be translated...." He calls it "an insult to the Word of God."[54]

The scholarly community has rendered its verdict on the NWT. The Society cannot blame the verdict on alleged Christian or "Trinitarian bias," for even non-Christian scholars of New Testament Greek agree that the NWT is inaccurate. They have arrived at this conclusion by means of rules of grammar, word meanings, and principles of translation that the Watchtower Society has blatantly violated.

14. What are some examples of NWT mistranslation?

The Watchtower Society has warned, "God does not deal with persons who ignore His Word and go according to their own independent ideas."[55] The Watchtower further asserts that Jehovah is against those who "steal" or change words from His Bible to make wrong applications.[56]

Yet the Watchtower has perpetrated just such error by incorporating hundreds of mistranslations in the NWT. Though space permits us to examine only a few examples of its mistranslations, even these make a mockery of the Society's claims to have tried to publish an honest, unbiased, accurate translation of the Bible.

In each of the examples below we will: a) list both the *New World Translation (NWT)* and the *New International*

Version (NIV) translations for comparison, b) give the Society's reason for mistranslating, and c) explain why the Jehovah's Witnesses' *New World Translation* is biased, dishonest and wrong.

Illustration 1—Titus 2:13

a) *Comparison of translations of Titus 2:13 (the same mistranslation occurs in 2 Peter 1:1).* The Jehovah's Witnesses in their *New World Translation* have translated Titus 2:13 in this way:

> NWT: "While we wait for the happy hope and glorious manifestation of the great God and of (the) Savior of us, Christ Jesus." (Jehovah's Witnesses have added the word *the* and put it in parentheses in front of the word Savior.)

On the other hand, the NIV translates this:

> NIV: "While we wait for the blessed hope—the glorious appearing of our great God and Savior, Jesus Christ...."

b) *The reason the Jehovah's Witnesses have mistranslated this verse is to deny the deity of Jesus Christ, a doctrine they do not accept.*

c) *Proof and documentation from scholars that the New World translators dishonestly translated this verse*:

By adding the word "the" in parentheses, the New World translators obscured the fact that in this verse Paul clearly called Jesus "our God and Savior." They have made it read as if Paul were speaking of two persons here, God and Jesus, rather than one, namely Jesus. Paul expressly stated that it is Jesus who is our great God and Savior. The Jehovah's Witnesses completely violate what Greek grammarians call Granville Sharp's rule for the use of the article with personal nouns in a series. In essence, Sharp's rule states that when two singular personal nouns (God and Savior) of the same case (God and Savior are both in the same case), are connected by "and" (the Greek word is *kai*), and the modifying article "the" (the Greek word is *ho*) appears only before the first noun, not before the second, both nouns must refer to the *same* person. In Titus 2:13, "God" and "Savior" are connected by "and." Also, "the" appears only before "God." Therefore, "God" and "Savior" must refer to the same Person—Jesus. (The same rule also applies to the words in 2 Peter 1:1 which the Jehovah's Witnesses have also mistranslated in the NWT.)

In fact, scholars have conclusively shown that in ancient times the phraseology "god and savior" was used of a ruling king, clearly showing that only one person was meant.[57] In an exhaustive study, C. Kuehne found Sharp's rule to be without demonstrable exception in the entire New Testament.[58] Thus, honest and unbiased scholarship requires that the words in these verses must be translated "our God and Savior, Jesus Christ." Dr. Bruce Metzger, an authority on the Greek language and professor at Princeton University, has stated:

> In support of this translation [our God and Savior must refer only to Jesus Christ] there may be quoted such eminent grammarians of the Greek New Testament as P. W. Schmiedel, J. H. Moulton, A. T. Robertson, and Blass-Debrunner. All of these scholars concur in the judgment that only one person is referred to in Titus 2:13 and that therefore, it must be rendered, "our great God and Savior, Jesus Christ."...[59]

Greek scholars Dana and Mantey, in their *A Manual Grammar of the Greek New Testament*, confirm the truth of Sharp's rule, and then explain: "Second Peter 1:1...means that Jesus is our God and Savior. After the same manner Titus 2:13...asserts that Jesus is the great God and Savior."[60] The greatest English-speaking Greek scholar, A. T. Robertson, insisted that "one person, *not* two, is in mind in 2 Peter 1:1."[61]

Even the context of Titus 2:13 shows that one Person, not two, was in Paul's mind, for Paul wrote of the "glorious appearing" of that Person. The Bible knows of only one such appearing: when "the Son of Man [Jesus] comes in his glory" (Luke 9:26). Indeed, an appearing of "the invisible God," other than as the visible Christ, who is His image (Colossians 1:15), would be impossible.

From all of this, scholars conclude that the Jehovah's Witnesses' *New World Translation* is a biased and inaccurate translation.

Illustration 2—Colossians 1:17

a) *Comparison of translations of Colossians 1:17.* The Jehovah's Witnesses in their NWT have translated Colossians 1:17 in this way (everyone agrees this verse speaks of Jesus):

> NWT: "Also, he is before all (other) things and by means of him all (other) things were made to exist." (The Jehovah's Witnesses have dishonestly inserted the word "other" twice and placed it in parentheses when this word does not appear at all in the Greek text.)

On the other hand, the NIV translates this:

> NIV: "He is before all things, and in him all things hold together."

b) *The reason why the Jehovah's Witnesses have mistranslated this verse is to change the fact that Christ is eternal and therefore God—a doctrine they deny.* To do so, they dishonestly insert a word not found in the original Greek language which gives the false impression that Christ Himself was a created being and not eternal.

c) *Proof and documentation that the New World translators dishonestly translated this verse:*

Here in Colossians 1:17 the Watchtower Society's translators have inserted the word "other" twice and put it in parentheses (they also did this three more times in verses 16 and 20). They did this to imply that Christ Himself is not the Creator. But as their own Greek interlinear shows (page 896), the Greek word *panta* means "all things," *not* "all other things."

The Watchtower claims that inserting "other" is justified five times because the context implies it. But the only thing that implies it is their own bias against Christ's deity.

The Watchtower Society's own Greek interlinear version (page 896) embarrasses them, for it proves that there is no "other" in the Greek text. Yet this didn't prevent earlier editions of the NWT from inserting "other" *without* parentheses or brackets, implying that it *was* part of the original Greek text (see the 1950 and 1953 editions). Even the 1965 edition of *Make Sure of All Things* quotes Colossians 1:15-20 in this manner, implying that "other" is actually in the Greek five different times.[62]

This is not the only place the Jehovah's Witnesses have added words to the text. Recent versions of the NWT have inserted the word "other" in Philippians 2:9 without parentheses or brackets, to change the meaning of that verse. The meaning is changed from "the name above every name" to "the name above every other name."

The Society's objectivity cannot be more questionable than in examples of this type. They add to the divine text what simply is not present in order to deny what clearly is taught.

One more example of how the NWT mistranslates the Bible is John 8:58. This verse is absolute proof that Jesus claimed to be God. Obviously, the Jehovah's Witnesses do not believe that, so they have deliberately and dishonestly changed the words. Instead of translating Jesus to say "...before Abraham was born, I am" (NIV), the Jehovah's Witnesses translated these words, "...before Abraham came into existence, I have been."

Christ's actual statement that He was the "I am" was clearly understood by the Jews to mean that Jesus had applied the divine name of God used in the Old Testament to Himself (Exodus 3:14; Isaiah 43:10). That is why the next verse states that the Jews immediately tried to stone Him to death for blasphemy (John 8:59).

The Jehovah's Witnesses have dishonestly translated Jesus' words "I am" to "I have been" to obscure the fact Jesus was making a direct claim to being God. In mistranslating these words, they try to teach that Jesus was saying He merely existed before as Michael the angel.

The Watchtower Society has explained its reason for translating the Greek *ego eimi* ("I am") as "I have been" in John 8:58. It's because the verb *eimi* is in the "perfect indefinite tense." But when scholars pointed out to them that there has never been a "perfect indefinite tense" in Greek and that *eimi*, as any beginner's Greek grammar shows, is the first person singular, present, active, indicative form of *einai*, "to be,"[63] and therefore it *must* be translated "I am," not "I have been," they changed their mind and gave a new reason for mistranslating this verse. This too was incorrect—nevertheless, the Society has even admitted once that it was the present indicative tense.[64] But it hasn't followed through and translated it as such in its English Bible. Only its theological bias can explain its blatant mistranslation. Interestingly, their *Kingdom Interlinear* which shows the Greek words actually condemns the Watchtower's translation, giving correctly "I am" directly beneath *ego eimi*. But unfortunately, no Jehovah's Witness will ever accept the truth of these words because the Watchtower translators further perpetuate this farce by placing "I have been" in the column to the right.[65]

Illustration 3—Matthew 25:46

a) *Comparison of translations of Matthew 25:46*. The Jehovah's Witnesses in their NWT have translated Matthew 25:46 in this way:

> NWT: "And these will depart into everlasting cutting-off, but the righteous ones into everlasting life."

On the other hand, the NIV translates this verse:

> NIV: "Then they will go away to eternal punishment, but the righteous to eternal life."

b) *The reason Jehovah's Witnesses have mistranslated this verse is to deny the biblical teaching on eternal punishment and replace it with their doctrine of the annihilation of the wicked.*

c) *Proof and documentation that the New World translators have mistranslated this verse:*

All standard Greek dictionaries define the Greek word in question in Matthew 25:46 (*kolasin*) as "punishment," not "cutting-off," as the Jehovah's Witnesses have claimed it means. The Watchtower is in conflict with standard Greek authorities, including: Moulton and Milligan's *The Vocabulary of the Greek New Testament* (Grand Rapids, MI: Eerdmans, 1980, p. 352), Thayer's *Greek-English Lexicon of the New Testament* (Grand Rapids, MI: Baker, 1983, p. 353), Walter Bauer's *Greek-English Lexicon of the New Testament and Other Early Christian Literature* (second edition, trans. William F. Arndt and F. Wilbur Gingrich, ed. F. W. Gingrich and Frederick W. Danker [Chicago: University of Chicago Press, 1979], p. 441), and Gerhard Kittel's *Theological Dictionary of the New Testament* (ten volumes, trans. Geoffrey W. Bromiley [Grand Rapids, MI: Eerdmans, 1978, vol. 3, p. 816]).

These authorities all say that the word *kolasin* must be translated as "punishment." This definition is clearly substantiated by the word's use around New Testament times. For example, one early Christian writing says that "evil-doers among men receive their reward not among the living only, but also await punishment (*kolasin*) and much torment (*basanon*)."[66] They could hardly suffer "torment" if they were annihilated, as the Watchtower Society believes.

Greek scholar Julius Mantey wrote that he had "found this word in first-century Greek writings in 107 different contexts, and in every one of them, it has the meaning of punishment, and never 'cutting-off.' "[67]

Another verse the Society mistranslates to support its rejection of the biblical doctrine of eternal punishment is Hebrews 9:27. The standard way this is understood can be seen from the NIV's translation which reads: "Just as man is destined to die once, and after that to face judgment...." Next, please notice how the NWT adds words not in the original to justify the Watchtower's own biased doctrine: "And as it is reserved for men to die *once for all time* [i.e., be annihilated], but after this a judgment." The words "for all time" are not in the Greek text, as their own interlinear shows (p. 988). Dr. Mantey observes, "No honest scholar would attempt to so pervert the word of God."[68] In the Bible God Himself warns all translators, "Do not add to His words, or He will rebuke you and prove you a liar" (Proverbs 30:6).

Space doesn't permit discussing all of the following verses, but consulting any of the standard authorities on New Testament Greek text will show in each instance that the NWT has dishonestly changed the true meaning of the words.

1) In Acts 20:28, the actual words "His own blood" have been mistranslated by the Watchtower Society as "the blood of His own (Son)" to circumvent Christ's deity.

2) In Hebrews 1:8, the proper translation, "Your throne, O God," has been mistranslated by the Watchtower Society to read, "God is your throne," in order to deny Christ's deity.

3) In Colossians 2:9, the word "deity" is mistranslated by the Watchtower Society as "divine quality," again in order to deny Christ's deity.

4) In John 1:1 the phrase, "the Word was God" is mistranslated by the Watchtower Society as "the Word was a god" to deny Christ's deity.

All of this clearly shows that the Watchtower Society miserably fails to pass the test of accurately translating the

Bible. Since the Watchtower's *New World Translation* has universally been condemned as a biased and inaccurate translation, then it cannot claim it is faithfully presenting the Word of God. And if it is not faithfully presenting the Word of God, the Watchtower Society cannot possibly be the sole channel on earth through which God has chosen to lead all men.

Distorting God's Word is serious enough. But making God a liar by speaking false prophecy in His name, so that men will worship a false god, is an offense so serious that in the Old Testament it brought the death penalty (Deuteronomy 13:1-5).

TEST TWO: If the Watchtower Society is the sole channel for God on earth, then according to the Bible its prophecy must come true. How reliable have its prophecies been?

---

15. What does the Watchtower Society teach and claim about prophecy?

In *The Watchtower*, Mar. 1, 1975, Jehovah's Witness leaders declared, "The Bible itself establishes the rules for testing a prophecy in Deuteronomy 18:20-23 and 13:1-8..." (p. 151). Its own rules, with which we agree, are biblical and are our standard; they demand 100 percent accuracy for any prophecy that is made. The Society's publication *Aid to Bible Understanding* teaches all Jehovah's Witnesses that prophecy includes "a declaration of something to come" and that "the source of all true prophecy is Jehovah God."[69] This publication further states that "correct understanding of prophecy would still be made available by God...particularly in the foretold 'time of the end'..." (p. 1346). (In context, "time of the end" here includes the emergence of the Watchtower Society.)

Aid to Bible Understanding further defines a "prophet" as "one through whom the divine will and purpose are made known" (p. 1347). (What's more, the Watchtower Society makes the astonishing claim that it is the true prophetic mouthpiece for God on earth at this time.)[70] Furthermore, the Watchtower tells all Jehovah's Witnesses that "the three essentials for establishing the credentials of the true prophet" are 1) speaking in Jehovah's name, 2) "the things foretold would come to pass," and 3) these prophecies would promote true worship by being in harmony with God's already-revealed Word. The Watchtower claims that the true prophet would "express...God's mind on matters... [and] every prediction [will be] related to God's will, purpose, standards or judgment."[71]

In light of these lofty claims, the Society has succinctly declared its position and authority. It claims to speak in the name of Jehovah, to be His prophet predicting future events, and to be in harmony with His Word. It confidently predicts that what it says must "come to pass." *The Watchtower*, Sept. 1, 1979, declared, "For nearly 60 years now the Jeremiah class [the Jehovah's Witnesses] have faithfully spoken forth Jehovah's word" (p. 29).

It is clear from this that the Watchtower Society confidently claims to prophetically speak for God. We will now examine some of the implications of its own claims to be speaking for God.

16. Has the Watchtower Society ever given false prophecies?

How have the predictions of the Watchtower Society stood the test of history? Let's look at a few. Frequently the Watchtower has attempted to predict the start of the Battle of Armageddon (the end of the world). (Unless otherwise noted, all quotations are from *The Watchtower*; dates appear at left.)[72] Let's look at a few predictions they have made in the name of God concerning the end of the world— what they often call Armageddon. (Because they believe Jesus has already returned invisibly, they look forward to the Battle of Armageddon, which they believe will usher in "paradise earth," not the Second Coming of Christ.) As you examine these prophecies, see if you really think that God spoke through them and gave the world the truth. Here are just a few of the predictions they have made through the years:

> In 1877 they said, "THE END OF THIS WORLD ...is nearer than most men suppose...."[73]
> In 1886 they said, "The *time* is come for Messiah to take the dominion of the earth...."[74]
> In 1889 they said, "...we present proofs that the setting up of the kingdom of God has already begun ...and that 'the battle of the great day of God almighty' (Revelation 16:14), which will end in AD 1914 with the complete overthrow of the earth's present rulership, is already commenced."[75] (In their 1915 edition of this same book they changed "AD 1914" to "AD 1915.")

On July 15, 1894 they said, "We see no reason for changing the figures—nor could we change them if we would. *They are, we believe, God's dates not ours* (emphasis added). But bear in mind that the end of 1914 is not the date for the *beginning*, but for the *end* of the time of trouble" (p. 1677 of *Reprints*, see note 72).

In 1904 they said, "The stress of the great time of trouble will be on us soon, somewhere between 1910 and 1912 culminating with the end of the 'times of the Gentiles,' October 1914."[76]

On May 1, 1914 they said, "There is absolutely no ground for Bible students to question that the consummation of this gospel age is now even at the door. . . . The great crisis . . . that will consume the ecclesiastical heavens and the social earth, is very near."[77]

But the year 1914 ended without a single one of these predictions coming true.[78]

In *Pastor Russell's Sermons* (1917, p. 676), Charles Taze Russell, founder and first president of the Jehovah's Witnesses, said of World War I, "The present great war in Europe is the beginning of the Armageddon of the Scriptures."

After Russell's death, "Judge" Rutherford continued the tradition of false prophecies given in the name and authority of God. He believed and stated that 1925 would mark the year of Christ's kingdom. He was wrong.[79] In *The Watchtower* magazine, Sept. 1, 1922, we find stated, "The date 1925 is even more distinctly indicated by the Scriptures because it is fixed by the law of God to Israel. . . . [One can see how] even before 1925 the great crisis will be reached and probably passed" (p. 262).

In *The Watchtower* magazine, Apr. 1, 1923, it stated, "Our thought is that 1925 is definitely settled by the Scriptures" (p. 106). But these and all other predictions proved false.

After utterly failing in the 1914 and 1925 predictions, finding many people leaving the Society, the leaders of the Watchtower became more cautious in setting dates. Nevertheless, they continued to hold out the promise of the imminency of Armageddon and the subsequent millennial kingdom. From 1930 to 1939 there were numerous declarations made about the future. For example:

In 1930 they said, "The great climax is at hand."[80]

In 1931 they said, "Armageddon is at hand...."[81]

In 1933 they said, "The incontrovertible proof that the time of deliverance is at hand."[82]

In 1933 they said, "That [Jehovah] has now opened these prophecies to the understanding of His anointed is evidence that the time of the battle is near; hence the prophecy is of profound interest to the anointed."[83]

In 1939 they said, "The battle of the great day of God Almighty is very near."[84]

In fact, from May, 1940, to April 15, 1943, just three short years, the Society made at least 44 predictions of the imminence of Armageddon.[85] Here are a few examples from this period and later:

In September, 1940, they said, "The kingdom is here, the king is enthroned. Armageddon is just ahead.... The great climax has been reached" (*The Messenger*, Sept. 1940, p. 6).

In *The Watchtower*, Sept. 15, 1941 they said, "The FINAL END IS VERY NEAR" (p. 276). "The remaining months before Armageddon..." (p. 288).

On January 15, 1942 they said, "The time is at hand for Jesus Christ to take possession of all things" (p. 28).

On May 1, 1942 they said, "Now, with Armageddon immediately before us..." (p. 139).

On May 1, 1943 they said, "The final end of all things... is at hand" (p. 139).

On September 1, 1944 they said, "Armageddon is near at hand" (p. 264).

In 1946, "The disaster of Armageddon... is at the door."[86]

In 1950 they said, "The March is on! Where? To the field of Armageddon for the 'war of the great day of God the Almighty.' "[87]

In 1953 they said, "Armageddon is so near at hand it will strike the generation now living."[88]

In 1955 they said, "It is becoming clear that the war of Armageddon is near its breaking out point."[89]

In 1958 they said, "When will Armageddon be fought?.... It will be very soon."[90]

These are just a few of the many false prophecies *The Watchtower* has made over the years. Is there any wonder the Jehovah's Witness leaders in their *Awake!* magazine, Oct. 8, 1968, p. 23, were forced to admit that "certain persons" had previously falsely predicted the end of the world? In this article Jehovah's Witness leaders asked why these false prophecies were given. Every Jehovah's Witness should take note of what they said. They said it was because they lacked God's guidance.

In this article in *Awake!* magazine (Oct. 8, 1968, p. 23) the Watchtower leadership admitted:

> True, there have been those in times past who predicted an "end to the world," even announcing a specific date. The "end" did not come. They were guilty of false prophesying. Why? What was missing?... Missing from such people were God's truths and the evidence that He was guiding and using them. But what about today? Today we have the evidence required, all of it, and it is overwhelming!

Notice that the Watchtower leaders have condemned themselves as false prophets. They admit that all through the years they were speaking in the name and authority of God, they were really lying and giving false prophecies.

If we accept that they gave false prophecies, God in Deuteronomy 18:20-22 says in the *New World Translation*:

> "However, the prophet who presumes to speak in my name a word that I have not commanded him to speak or who speaks in the name of other gods, that prophet must die. And in case you should say in your heart: 'How shall we know the word that Jehovah has not spoken?' When the prophet speaks in the name of Jehovah and the word does not occur or come true, that is the word that Jehovah did not speak. With presumptuousness the prophet spoke it. You must not get frightened at him."

But in spite of their tragic record of predictions that did not come to pass, they disregarded the Word of God in Deuteronomy 18 and as the above quote from *Awake!* magazine shows, they confidently asked the people to believe that now they would speak for God in predicting the future. They now began to strongly imply it would be the year 1975 in which Armageddon would occur.[91]

> In 1973 they said, "The 'Great Tribulation' is very near."[92]
> In 1973 they said, "According to the Bible's timetable, the beginning of the seventh millennium of

mankind's existence on earth is near at hand, within this generation."[93]

In *Kingdom Ministry*, May, 1974, the world's end was said to be "so very near" that Jehovah's Witnesses were commended who sold "their homes and property" to devote themselves to full-time service in "the short time remaining before the wicked world's end" (p. 3).

> In 1975 they said, "The fulfillment . . . is immediately ahead of us."[94]
> In 1975 they said, "Very short must be the time that remains. . . ."[95]

Many Jehovah's Witnesses living today can remember when the year 1975 came and went, bringing great discouragement to the faithful and providing further embarrassment to the Watchtower Society.

But the charade still continued. From 1976 to 1981 the Society repeatedly said that Armageddon was "very near," "at hand," etc. And from 1981 to the present the Society still claims that the world is near its end.

It is said that Jehovah's Witnesses believe that the Watchtower's authoritative statements are true and genuinely reflect God's guidance. But if the Society has been indisputably wrong in every period, how can modern Witnesses trust it? Would any employer rehire a thief for the tenth time after nine offenses? The answer is no. Thousands of Jehovah's Witnesses have left the Watchtower after having lived through the high expectations and heartbreaking disappointments of these false prophecies. Thousands more have left who investigated these false prophecies in the Watchtower literature.

Still, the Watchtower Society claims that Jehovah's Witnesses' "unswerving attention to such inspired prophecy has held them true to the right course till now."[96] After reading its false prophecies through the years and its own admission that it lied, what do you think?

The Society still claims of Armageddon, "Jehovah has His own fixed date for its arrival."[97] The Watchtower has missed that date every time it has predicted it.

17. Does the Watchtower Society admit to false prophecy?

Jehovah's Witnesses have admitted serious errors. In their official Watchtower publication, *Man's Salvation* (1975), they now admit that Charles Taze Russell was wrong in his 1874 prediction of Christ's second coming.[98] They admit that they were wrong in their 1914 prediction.[99] They admit that they were wrong in their prediction of 1925.[100] They admit that they were wrong about their prediction in 1975.[101]

Yet in that same year in their *1975 Yearbook* they claim that for over a century "Jehovah's servants" have "enjoyed spiritual enlightenment and direction."[102] What do you think? Does the evidence show they have passed the second test they themselves laid down, namely that any prophecy given in the name of God must come true? Have their prophecies come true 100 percent of the time?[103] If not, can the Watchtower Society claim it is God's sole channel of communication to men on earth today?

TEST THREE: If the Watchtower Society is God's sole channel for communication on earth, then its scholarship should be trustworthy—but is it?

---

18. Has the Watchtower Society ever lied, covered up and changed important doctrines, dates, and Bible interpretations?

If God actually speaks to all men through the Watchtower Society—giving prophecy, Bible interpretations, and other instruction—in looking at the Watchtower materials, it appears He must change His mind a great deal. These words and our question sound blunt, but we are only doing what Judge Rutherford told us to do for the Jehovah's Witnesses. He said in *The Golden Age*, Jan. 18, 1933, p. 252:

> If the message Jehovah's Witnesses are bringing to the people is true, then it is of greatest importance to mankind. If it is false then it is the duty of the clergymen and others who support them to come boldly forward and plainly tell the people wherein the message is false.

The fact is, the Watchtower Society leaders have lied and covered up important material. Even *The Watchtower*, June 1, 1960, p. 352, encourages "hiding the truth from God's enemies." They say it is proper to deceive people (God's enemies) but they claim this is not lying. This is because they have a different definition of lying as stated in their text *Aid to Bible Understanding*, p. 1060, where they say that lying "generally involves saying something false to a person who is *entitled* to know the truth...." The fact is, however, it is not just "God's enemies" they have lied to, but their own people.

Here are a few of the changes in dates, prophecies, and its doctrines that the Watchtower Society has made through the years. What is so condemning is that all of this can be found in its own authoritative writings.

For example, 1) The Watchtower Society changed the beginning of the "time of the end" from the date 1799 to 1914; 2) it changed the second coming of Christ from the date 1874 to 1914; 3) it changed the entire nature of the second coming of Christ from an earthly and visible return to a heavenly and invisible return; 4) it changed the time of the "first resurrection" from the date 1878 to 1914; 5) it changed the date of the termination of the 6000 years of creation from the year 1872 to 1972 and then once again to 1975.[104] Why so many changes? Simple: The predicted events didn't happen. The changes were made to cover up its false prophecies to hide the fact that God really hadn't spoken through it.

Next, here are a few changes the Watchtower Society has made concerning important doctrines. 1) The Watchtower Society changed its doctrine concerning life-saving vaccination from commands rejecting it to permission to accept it; 2) the Watchtower changed the identity of the "Faithful and Wise Servant" from Charles Taze Russell, its first president, to the Watchtower Society itself; 3) the Watchtower Society once said the book of Ruth should be interpreted as history, but later changed and said it should be read as prophecy; 4) the Watchtower changed the identity of "Abaddon" in Revelation 11, first saying this angel was Satan, and later saying this was Jesus Christ; 5) the Watchtower in its early years accepted blood transfusions, but then made rejection of blood transfusions a key doctrine; 6) the Watchtower first accepted the worship of Jesus, but now rejects the worship of Jesus; 7) the Watchtower changed the doctrine concerning the resurrection of the dead—first *all* were to be raised, now only some were to be raised; 8) it changed its view of Israel—from literal (a physical nation) to spiritual (all believers); 9) the Watchtower changed the definition of the "superior authorities" found in Romans 13 from political rulers on earth to God and Jesus in heaven, and then back again to political rulers on earth.[105]

With all these changes one wonders, "Can the average Witness know that what he is told is true today won't be declared false tomorrow?" Former Jehovah's Witness Edmond Gruss in his standard text *Apostles of Denial* documents that "thousands of reinterpretations of Scripture" and many new doctrinal points developed after Russell's death; he cites many illustrations.[106] Former Witness William J. Schnell notes, "I had observed *The Watchtower* magazine change our doctrines between 1917 and 1928 no less than 148 times . . ."[107] One example is Luke 16:19-31 which has been interpreted in five different ways.[108] How, then, can the average Jehovah's Witness know God's true mind on any passage of Scripture?[109]

These are only a sample of the changes the Watchtower Society has made in the name of God concerning its Bible interpretation, its doctrine, and its prophetic dates. Do its statements support the claim that the Watchtower Society "from the time of its organization until now" has been God's sole "collective channel for the flow of biblical truth to men on earth?" Do its false prophecies support the claim that for over a century Jehovah's servants have "enjoyed spiritual enlightenment and direction?"[110] One wonders how the Watchtower Society could say "Jehovah never makes any mistakes,"[111] since it also claims Jehovah is speaking through it? In the Bible, God Himself clearly states He is the "God of truth" who "cannot lie" (Psalm 31:5; Titus 1:2). Indeed, "it is impossible for God to lie" for "no lie is of the truth" (Hebrews 6:18; 1 John 2:21). God does not make mistakes concerning dates nor change His mind on doctrinal matters. Is there any other conclusion we can come to except that the Watchtower Society has misled millions of people in claiming it alone is God's sole channel of communication on earth today?

TEST FOUR: If the Watchtower Society admits it receives much of its teachings from angels or spirits and those teachings have proven to be false—is such a source trustworthy?

---

19. Has the Watchtower Society ever claimed to receive information from angels or spirits?

It can be documented that the Watchtower Society in its early years dabbled in the occult,[112] although the Society's official position toward occult activity is supposedly in agreement with the prohibition found in Deuteronomy 18:9-12. Nevertheless, today the Watchtower Society appears to be unsuspectingly involved in the occult in at least one

38

manner: It seems to accept demonic guidance and revelations which come to it in the disguise of angelic or spiritistic contacts.

The Watchtower in the past has claimed "angelic guidance" for its Bible translators in their writing of Jehovah's Witnesses' doctrine and practice. If real supernatural activity has occurred, and the Watchtower's translation, doctrines and practices have failed to meet biblical, moral,[113] and scholarly standards, it seems hardly likely that the supernatural assistance was from God. Godly angels would never lend help to an organization that denies the true nature of who God is, deliberately distorts His word, and completely rejects His Son. But the Bible says fallen angels—demons—would. The Bible further declares that demons masquerade as "angels of light" while doing so (2 Corinthians 11:14).

Besides the Watchtower Society's express claim (p. 21) that "angels" guided its translators in translating the *New World Translation* of the Bible, former service department member Bill Cetnar in the Jehovah's Witnesses headquarters at Brooklyn, New York, found many Watchtower beliefs were also professed by a spirit-possessed medium the Society was quoting.[114]

"Judge" Rutherford openly stated that angels helped write *The Watchtower* magazine when he said "the Lord through His angel sees to it that the information is given to His people in due time. . . ."[115] The current worldwide president of Jehovah's Witnesses is F. W. Franz who also speaks of angels guiding the Watchtower. He has said, "We believe that the angels of God are used in directing Jehovah's Witnesses."[116]

Among other things *The Watchtower* claims that angels enlighten and comfort, bring refreshing truths, and transmit information to "God's anointed people."[117] In another clear statement of its belief that angels guide the leaders of Jehovah's Witnesses, we read in *The Watchtower* magazine, "Jehovah's Witnesses today make their declaration of the good news of the kingdom under angelic direction and support."[118]

In *The Watchtower*, Dec. 1, 1981 (p. 27), and July 15, 1960 (p. 439), the leaders of the Jehovah's Witnesses claim to be God's "channel of communication," actively "channeling" (the use of this common New Age term is theirs) since the days of Rutherford. In the issue of Apr. 1, 1972 (p. 200), they claim that all spiritual direction is supplied by invisible angels. In the issues of Nov. 15, 1933 (p. 344),

Nov. 1, 1935 (p. 331), and Dec. 15, 1987 (p. 7), they claim that the name "Jehovah's Witnesses" and their key doctrine of "Christ's" invisible return in 1914 were channeled by invisible angels.

Under the second president of the Jehovah's Witnesses, "Judge" Rutherford, the Witnesses received most of their basic doctrines. Yet Rutherford believed that God's "holy spirit" had ceased to function as his teacher and had been replaced by angels who taught him in his mind (*The Watchtower*, Sept. 1, 1930, p. 263, and Feb. 1, 1935, p. 41; Rutherford, *Riches* [1936], p. 316).

Today the Society's leaders claim that both "holy spirit" and "angels" communicate information to them (*The Watchtower*, Mar. 1, 1972, p. 155; Aug. 1, 1987, p. 19).[119]

In conclusion, these rather startling admissions from the Watchtower documenting that it receives information and guidance from "angels" coupled with the fact of all its false prophecies, biased Bible translation, and unbiblical teachings lead us to believe it is receiving its information from demons rather than from God.

CONCLUSION

20. What can you do if you are a Jehovah's Witness who desires to live for God and Christ and yet are unsure about what you have been taught?

First, if you are a Jehovah's Witness, don't be discouraged. Don't give up on God because someone lied to you. Perhaps you accepted the Watchtower's claims without first testing them carefully. Possibly your own doubts and discouragement will become the means by which God leads you into the truth and into a personal relationship with Him.

Second, realize that you aren't alone. Former worldwide Governing Body board member Raymond Franz estimates that between 1970 and 1979 over 750,000 Jehovah's Witnesses were disfellowshipped or left the Watchtower organization.[120]

Third, take the initiative: Get at the truth for yourself. The Watchtower has told you before that "sincere seekers for the truth want to know what is right."[121] If you study the Bible on your own, in humility before God, God says He Himself will show you the truth:

"But if any of you lacks wisdom, let him ask of God, who gives to all men generously and

> without reproach, and it will be given to Him.
> ... Draw near to God and He will draw near to
> you" (James 1:5; 4:8).

Ask Him, and He'll help you. Believe and obey His Word, don't alter it, and you will know the truth and as Jesus promised "the truth will make you free" (John 8:31,32).

Fourth, accept God's loving and free gift of salvation in Christ Jesus (no works to earn it!). God never intended for you to spend your life in a hopeless, never-ending attempt to earn your own salvation by measuring up to His standard of perfection. He has already told us it's impossible for any person to do so. Because of your fallen nature, you'll never be able to do it (Romans 8:3). "But because of His great love for us, God, who is rich in mercy, made us alive with Christ even when we were dead in transgressions—it is by grace you have been saved" (Ephesians 2:4,5 cf. Romans 8:3). The really good news that God gives to all of us is:

"Therefore, there is now no condemnation for those who are in Christ Jesus" (Romans 8:1).

"You see, at just the right time, when we were still powerless, Christ died for the ungodly" (Romans 5:6).

"But the gift of God is eternal life in Christ Jesus our Lord" (Romans 6:23).

"However, to the man who does not work [for salvation] but trusts God who justifies the wicked, his faith is credited as righteousness" (Romans 4:5).

"So we, too, have put our faith in Christ Jesus that we may be justified by faith in Christ and not by observing the law, because by observing the law no one will be justified.... I do not set aside the grace of God, for if righteousness could be gained through the law, Christ died for nothing!" (Galatians 2:16,21)

Fifth, God wants you to confess your sins and accept the forgiveness He provided through Christ's shed blood. Read Isaiah 55:1-3 and see how eagerly God longs for you to come to Him to rest. Do you long for eternal life? God's Word says you can *know* that you have it:

> The one who believes in the Son of God has
> the witness in himself; the one who does not
> believe God has made Him a liar, because he has
> not believed in the witness that God has borne
> concerning His Son. And the witness is this,
> that God has *given* us eternal life, and this life is
> in His Son. *He who has the Son has the life*; he
> who does not have the Son of God *does not* have

the life. These things I have written to you who believe in the name of the Son of God, in order that *you may know that you have eternal life* (1 John 5:10-13, emphasis added).

You can receive the gift of salvation, and know that you have eternal life, right now, by praying sincerely:

> "Dear God, I'm confused. But I long to know You and serve You as You really are. Please reveal Yourself to me. I confess that I'm a sinner and incapable of earning merit in Your eyes. I believe Jesus' words, "You must be born again." I now receive Jesus Christ as my personal Lord and Savior. I receive Him as my God. I commit myself to Him and to Your Word. Please help me to understand it correctly. Amen."

RECOMMENDED READING

General Critical Treatments
(Starred texts contain photo documentation of rare documents.)

*Duane Magnani, *Point/Counterpoint: A Refutation of the Jehovah's Witnesses' Book Reasoning From the Scriptures, Vol. 1: False Prophets* (Clayton, CA: P. O. Box 597, Witness, Inc.). Witness, Inc., carries a large number of important critical works on the Witnesses in the area of history, doctrine, and morality. See their publications list.

Danger at Your Door (Clayton, CA: Witness, Inc., 1987).

Dialogue With Jehovah's Witnesses (Clayton, CA: Witness, Inc., 1987).

Raymond Franz, *Crisis of Conscience* (USA: Commentary Press), 1983.

Edmond Gruss, *Apostles of Denial: An Examination and Exposé of the History, Doctrines and Claims of the Jehovah's Witnesses* (Grand Rapids, MI: Baker).

On The New World Translation

Robert H. Countess, *The Jehovah's Witnesses' New Testament: A Critical Analysis of the New World Translation of the Christian Greek Scriptures* (Phillipsburg, NJ: Presbyterian & Reformed, 1987).

Prophecy

Edmond Gruss, *The Jehovah's Witnesses and Prophetic Speculation* (Nutley, NJ: Presbyterian & Reformed, 1972).

Carl Olof Jonsson, *The Gentile Times Reconsidered* (La Jolla, CA: Good News Defenders, 1983).

On the Doctrine of the Trinity

E. Calvin Beisner, *God in Three Persons* (Wheaton, IL: Tyndale House, 1984).

Edward Henry Bickersteth, *The Trinity* (Grand Rapids, MI: Kregel, 1976).

Robert Glenn Gromacki, *The Virgin Birth: Doctrine of Deity* (Nashville, TN: Thomas Nelson, 1974). [Reprinted as *The Virgin Birth of Christ* (Baker, 1981).]

NOTES

(Note: Most Jehovah's Witnesses' materials are published anonymously by the Watchtower Bible and Tract Society [WBTS], Brooklyn, NY. Few are listed with a specific author. See note 72.)

1. Edmond Gruss, *Apostles of Denial: An Examination and Exposé of the History, Doctrines and Claims of the Jehovah's Witnesses* (Grand Rapids, MI: Baker, 1972), pp. 14-16.
2. C. J. Woodworth and George H. Fisher, comp. and ed., *The Finished Mystery*, Volume 7 of *Studies in the Scriptures*, 1918 ed. (Brooklyn, NY: International Bible Students Assoc., 1917), p. 387; cited in Gruss, op. cit., p. 21.
3. *The Watchtower*, Sept. 15, 1910, p. 298, from, Chicago Bible Students, *Reprints of the Original Watchtower and Herald of Christ's Presence*, 12 volumes plus index (Chicago, IL: Chicago Bible Students), n.d.
4. *The Watchtower*, Aug. 15, 1981, pp. 28-29.
5. See Gruss, op cit., Chapter 5.
6. Ibid., p. 76.
7. Raymond Franz, *Crisis of Conscience* (Atlanta, GA: Commentary, 1983), pp. 345, 347, 354, 290-291, 303, 25-26, 51, 137-139, 147-148, 164-223, 9-10, 16, 41, 47, 238-239, 344, 52-65, 195, 29-52, 97, 245, 257.
8. *Life Everlasting in the Freedom of the Sons of God* (WBTS, 1966), p. 181.
9. Edmond Gruss, *We Left Jehovah's Witnesses—A Non-Prophet Organization* (Nutley, NJ: Presbyterian & Reformed, 1974), p. 78.
10. *The Watchtower*, Mar. 1, 1979, p. 16.
11. *The Watchtower*, July 15, 1960, p. 439, cited in Michael Van Buskirk, *The Scholastic Dishonesty of the Watchtower* (Santa Ana, CA: CARIS, 1976), p. 26.
12. H. Montague, "Watchtower Congregations: Communion or Conflict?" (Costa Mesa, CA: CARIS), p. 7. See Duane Magnani, *The Watchtower Files: Dialogue With a Jehovah's Witness* (Minneapolis, MN: Bethany Fellowship, 1985), p. 17, for documentation from court records of a statement by Nathan H. Knorr that *The Watchtower* is the word of God "without any qualification whatsoever."
13. Gruss, *We Left Jehovah's Witnesses*, op. cit., p. 41.
14. *You Can Live Forever in Paradise on Earth* (WBTS, 1982), p. 212.
15. *Blood, Medicine and the Law of God* (WBTS, 1961), p. 55. Cited in Duane Magnani and Arthur Barrett, *Dialogue With Jehovah's Witnesses*, two volumes (Witness, Inc., P.O. Box 597, Clayton, CA, 1983), Vol. 2, p. 371.

15a. William and Joan Cetnar, *Questions For Jehovah's Witnesses* (William J. Cetnar: R.D. #3, Kunkletown, PA, 1983), p. 26; Duane Magani, *Dialogue With a Jehovah's Witness* (Clayton, CA: Witness, Inc.), Vol. 2, pp. 368-374. For a refutation of this view, see Jerry Bergman, *Jehovah's Witnesses and Blood Transfusions* (St. Louis, MO: Personal Freedom Outreach), n.d.; Martin, note 21, pp. 91-105.

16. *Man's Salvation Out of World Distress at Hand!* (WBTS, 1975), p. 335.

17. *The Watchtower*, Sept. 1, 1979, p. 21.

18. J. F. Rutherford, *Preparation* (WBTS, 1933), pp. 19-20.

19. J. F. Rutherford, *Religion* (WBTS, 1940), p. 104. Cited in Gruss, *Apostles of Denial*, op. cit., p. 63.

20. *The Watchtower*, Sept. 1, 1979, p. 8.

21. *The Watchtower*, Oct. 1, 1952, pp. 596-604. Cited in Walter R. Martin, *Jehovah of the Watchtower* (Chicago: Moody Press, rev. ed. 1974), p. 109.

22. C. T. Russell, *Studies in the Scriptures*, Volume 7: *The Finished Mystery*, p. 410. Cited in W. M. Nelson and R. K. Smith, "Jehovah's Witnesses, Part 2, Their Mission," in David Hesselgrave, ed., *Dynamic Religious Movements: Case Studies of Rapidly Growing Religious Movements Around the World* (Grand Rapids, MI: Baker, 1978), p. 181.

23. *Aid to Bible Understanding* (WBTS, 1971), p. 665; Duane Magnani, *The Heavenly Weatherman* (Clayton, CA: Witness, Inc., 1987), pp. 1-8, 42-50, 246-51, etc.

24. *Then Is Finished the Mystery of God* (WBTS, 1969), p. 10.

25. J. F. Rutherford, *Uncovered* (WBTS, 1937), pp. 48-49. Cited in Charles S. Braden, *These Also Believe: A Study of Modern American Cults and Minority Religious Movements* (NY: Macmillan, 1970), p. 371. *Let God Be True* (WBTS, 1976), p. 82, states, "Satan is the originator of the 'Trinity' doctrine."

26. *Let God Be True* (WBTS, 1946), p. 83; *Things in Which It Is Impossible for God to Lie* (WBTS, 1965), p. 259; *The Watchtower*, July, 1982, pp. 2-3.

27. The verses listed with each of these five points should be read in a good, modern translation like the *New International Version* or the *New American Standard Bible*, since some were mistranslated in the *King James Version* and in the NWT. See Question 13 & 14.

28. For an indepth study of the historical development of the doctrine of the Trinity from apostolic times through the final form of the Nicene Creed adopted at the Council of Constantinople in A.D. 381, including a line-by-line comparison of the Creed with New Testament teaching, see E. Calvin Beisner, *God in Three Persons* (Wheaton, IL: Tyndale House, 1984).

29. *Is This Life All There Is?* (WBTS, 1974), p. 99.

30. C. T. Russell, *Studies in the Scriptures, Volume 5: The Atonement Between God and Man* (East Rutherford, NJ: Dawn Bible Students Assoc., reprint of 1899 ed.), n.d., p. 60.

31. *Aid to Bible Understanding*, op. cit., p. 1152.

32. *The Watchtower*, Aug. 22, 1976, pp. 25-26; *Aid to Bible Understanding*, op. cit., p. 918.

33. *Let God Be True*, 1946, op. cit., p. 65.

34. *The Watchtower*, Aug. 15, 1976, p. 495. cf. *The Watchtower*, May 15, 1932, p. 155; Nov. 1, 1919, p. 332-333.

35. C. T. Russell, *Studies in the Scriptures, Vol. 5: The Atonement Between God and Man*, op. cit., p. 454. cf. note 36.

36. *The Truth Shall Make You Free* (WBTS, 1943), p. 264; Hoekema, op. cit., p. 272; James Bjornstad, *Counterfeits at Your Door* (Glendale, CA: Regal, 1979), pp. 67-68, 92-94; Nelson and Smith in Hesselgrave, op. cit., pp. 178-179; *Things in Which it is Impossible For God to Lie*, op. cit., p. 219; *Let Your Name Be Sanctified* (WBTS, 1961), p. 272; *Man's Salvation Out of World Distress at Hand!*, (WBTS, 1975) pp. 42-43; *The Watchtower*, Jan. 15, 1980, p. 31; *Make Sure of All Things, Hold Fast to What Is Fine* (WBTS, 1965), p. 255.

37. *Reasoning From the Scriptures* (WBTS, 1985), pp. 95-98. However, in *Studies in the Scriptures, Volume 4: The Battle of Armageddon*, op. cit., p. 621, Russell wrote, "Our Lord, the appointed King, is now present, since October 1874, A.D., according to the testimony of the prophets, to those who have ears to hear it...."

38. See *Aid to Bible Understanding*, op. cit., p. 437 and the discussion in Anthony Hoekema, *The Four Major Cults* (Eerdmans, 1970), pp. 279-285.

39. *Reasoning From the Scriptures*, op. cit., pp. 76-77.

40. *You May Survive Armageddon into God's New World* (WBTS, 1955), op. cit., p. 356.

41. The Witnesses may in places define God's grace properly, but they do not live as if it were true. See Gruss, *We Left Jehovah's Witnesses, a Non-Prophet Organization*, op. cit, pp. 131-132; Magnani, *Watchtower Files*, op. cit., Chapter 13.

42. *Making Your Family Life Happy* (WBTS, 1978), pp. 182-183.

43. *The Watchtower*, May 1, 1979, p. 20; cf. *The Watchtower*, May 1, 1980, p. 13; also Aug. 1, 1981, p. 20.

44. *Life Everlasting in the Freedom of the Sons of God*, op. cit. p. 400.

45. *Aid to Bible Understanding*, op. cit., p. 437; *You May Survive Armageddon into God's New World*, op. cit., pp. 356-357; Gruss, *We Left Jehovah's Witnesses, a Non-Prophet Organization*, op. cit., pp. 131-132.

46. Discussions with members, former members, and *Reasoning From the Scriptures*, op. cit., p. 277.

47. *All Scripture is Inspired By God and Beneficial*, (WBTS, 1963), pp. 326, 327-30.

48. *The New World Translation of the Holy Scriptures* (WBTS, 1961), p. 5.

49. *The Kingdom Interlinear Translation of the Greek Scriptures* (WBTS, 1969), p. 5; *Reasoning From the Scriptures*, op. cit., p. 277, states: "We have not used any scholar's name for reference or recommendations because...the translation must be appraised on its own merits."

50. Cited in Gruss, *Apostles of Denial*, op. cit., pp. 32-33, 219; Gruss has seen the original court transcripts himself. This is a rather startling admission, for the control of men by spirits sounds more like demonism than divine inspiration. One mediumistic translator of the Bible, who claimed that his translation originated in the spirit world, handled several passages similarly to how the Society handles them. The 1937 New Testament translation by occult medium Johannes Greber translates John 1:1, Hebrews 1:8, and other passages the way the NWT does. Indeed, the Society quotes Greber's translation to support its own. See note 114. If indeed translators were "controlled by angels of various ranks," it was by unholy angels—demons. Only then would they have so twisted the translation. For documentation as to parallels between the NWT and this mediumistic translation, see William and Joan Cetnar, *Questions for Jehovah's Witnesses*, op. cit., pp. 48-55.

51. Julius Mantey, *Depth Exploration in the New Testament* (NY: Vantage Press, 1980), pp. 136-137.

52. Bruce M. Metzger, "The Jehovah's Witnesses and Jesus Christ: A Biblical and Theological Appraisal," Rpt. of *Theology Today* article, April 1953 (Princeton, NJ: Theological Book Agency), p. 74.

53. Robert Countess, *The Jehovah's Witnesses' New Testament: A Critical Analysis of the New World Translation of the Christian Greek Scriptures* (Phillipsburg, NJ: Presbyterian & Reformed, 1987), pp. 91,93.

54. H. H. Rowley, "How Not to Translate the Bible," *The Expository Times*, Nov. 1953, pp. 41-42; cf. Jan., 1956, cited by Gruss, *Apostles of Denial*, op. cit., pp. 212-213.

55. *The Watchtower*, Mar. 15, 1972, p. 189.

56. *The Watchtower*, Sept. 1, 1979, p. 30.

57. A. T. Robertson, *A Grammar of the Greek New Testament in the Light of Historical Research* (Nashville, TN: Broadman Press, 1934), p. 786.

58. C. Kuehne, "The Greek Article and the Doctrine of Christ's Deity," *Journal of Theology*, Church of the Lutheran Confession, Vol. 13, Nos. 3-4, Vol. 14, Nos. 1-4, Sept. 1973-Dec. 1974. Cited in the CARIS *Newsletter* (P.O. Box 1783, Santa Ana, CA), May, 1978, Vol. 2, No. 2. (Condensed version by Michael Van Buskirk endorsed as accurate by Kuehne; "Letters," CARIS *Newsletter* op. cit., Vol. 2, No. 3.)

59. Metzger, op. cit., p. 79.

60. H. E. Dana and Julius R. Mantey, *A Manual Grammar of the Greek New Testament* (Toronto: Macmillan, 1957), p. 147.

61. A. T. Robertson, *Word Pictures in the New Testament*, six volumes (Nashville, TN: Broadman, 1933), Vol. 6, p. 147.

62. *Make Sure of All Things*, op. cit., p. 364.

63. See, for example, Alston Hurd Chase and Henry Phillips, Jr., *A New Introduction to Greek*, third ed. (Cambridge, MA: Harvard University Press, 1972), p. 41.

64. The Society has given four *different* grammatical constructions for *ego eimi*. See Michael Van Buskirk, *The Scholastic Dishonesty of the Watchtower* (Santa Ana, CA: CARIS, 1976), p. 20.

65. *The Kingdom Interlinear Translation of the Greek Scriptures*, op. cit., p. 467.

66. James Hope Moulton and William Milligan, *The Vocabulary of the Greek Testament* (Grand Rapids, MI: Eerdmans, 1976), p. 352, citing from B. P. Grenfell and A. S. Hunt, eds., *The Oxyrhynchus Papyri* (London: 1898-1927), Vol. 5, p. 840.

67. Mantey, *Depth Exploration in the New Testament*, op. cit., p. 142.

68. Ibid., p. 143.

69. *Aid to Bible Understanding*, op. cit., p. 1344.

70. *The Watchtower*, July 1, 1943, p. 203; Mar. 15, 1971, p. 189, Apr. 1, 1972, p. 197, Jan. 15, 1959, pp. 40-41; *The Nations Shall Know That I Am Jehovah—How?* (Brooklyn, NY: WBTS, 1971), pp. 58, 70-71.

71. *Aid to Bible Understanding*, op. cit., p. 1348.

72. Reprints of early editions of *The Watchtower* are available in *Reprints of the Original Watchtower and Herald of Christ's Presence*, 1879-1916 (Vols. 1-12), from Chicago Bible Students, Box 6016, Chicago, IL 60680.

73. N. H. Barbour and C. T. Russell, *Three Worlds and the Harvest of This World* (Rochester: Barbour and Russell, 1877), p. 17; cited in Gruss, *The Jehovah's Witnesses and Prophetic Speculation* (Nutley, NJ: Presbyterian & Reformed, 1972), p. 82.

74. *Zion's Watchtower and Herald of Christ's Presence*, January, 1886, p. 1 (*Reprints*, Vol. 2, p. 817. See note 72).

75. C. T. Russell, *The Time Is at Hand* (Allegheny, PA: WBTS, 1889), p. 101; cited in Gruss, *Jehovah's Witnesses and Prophetic Speculation*, op. cit., p. 83.

76. C. T. Russell, *The New Creation* (WBTS, 1904), p. 579; cited in Gruss, ibid., p. 84.

77. *The Watchtower*, May 1, 1914, p. 134 (*Reprints* p. 5450).

78. Ibid., pp. 23-26.

79. J. F. Rutherford, *Millions Now Living Will Never Die* (WBTS, 1920), pp. 97, 105, 140; Gruss, ibid., p. 87.

80. J. F. Rutherford, *Light* (WBTS, 1930), Vol. 2, p. 327; cited in Gruss, ibid., p. 89.

81. J. F. Rutherford, *Vindication* (WBTS, 1931), Vol. 1, p. 147.

82. J. F. Rutherford, *Preparation*, op. cit., p. 11.

83. Ibid., pp. 16-18.

84. J. F. Rutherford, *Salvation* (WBTS, 1939), p. 310; cited in Gruss, *Jehovah's Witnesses and Prophetic Speculation*, op. cit., p. 89.

85. Copies on file. Thanks to Professor Edmond C. Gruss for supplying them.

86. *Let God Be True* (WBTS, 1946), p. 194.

87. *This Means Everlasting Life* (WBTS, 1950), p. 311; cited in Gruss, *Jehovah's Witnesses and Prophetic Speculation*, op. cit., p. 93.

88. *You May Survive Armageddon Into God's New World*, op. cit., p. 11, cf. p. 362. This statement is from a speech given in 1953.

89. Ibid., p. 331.

90. *From Paradise Lost to Paradise Regained* (WBTS, 1958), p. 205.

91. See the discussion with photo documentation in Magnani, *Dialogue with a Jehovah's Witness*, op. cit., Vol 2, pp. 53-55 and Gruss, *The Jehovah's Witnesses and Prophetic Speculation*, op. cit., pp. 13-15; *Then is Finished the Mystery of God* (WBTS, 1969), pp. 364-371.

92. *True Peace and Security—From What Source?* (WBTS, 1973), p. 83.

93. *God's Kingdom of a Thousand Years Has Approached*, (WBTS, 1973), p. 44.

94. *Man's Salvation Out of World Distress at Hand*, op. cit., p. 312.

95. Ibid., p. 349.

96. Ibid., pp. 283-284.

97. Ibid., p. 309.

98. Ibid., p. 287. Under oath, legal counsel for the Society, Hayden C. Covington also admitted the prophecy was false, and that it nevertheless had to be accepted by Witnesses to preserve "unity at all costs." See transcript in Gruss, *The Jehovah's Witnesses and Prophetic Speculation*, op. cit., pp. 99-101.

99. *1975 Yearbook of Jehovah's Witnesses* (WBTS, 1974), p. 76.

100. Ibid., pp. 145-146.

101. *1980 Yearbook of Jehovah's Witnesses* (WBTS, 1979), pp. 30-31.

102. *1975 Yearbook of Jehovah's Witnesses*, op. cit., p. 245.

103. Additional documentation of false prophecies and the Watchtower Society's suppression of vital information can be found in Gruss, *The Jehovah's Witnesses and Prophetic Speculation*, op. cit., and in former 25-year member Carl Olof Jonsson's *The Gentile Times Reconsidered* (La Jolla, CA: Good News Defenders, 1983).

104. Gruss, *Apostles of Denial*, op. cit., pp. 232-234, citing original documentation.

105. William and Joan Cetnar, op. cit., p. 30. All but the first illustration are taken from Gruss, *We Left Jehovah's Witnesses: A Non-Prophet Organization*, op. cit., pp. 156-159, citing original documentation.

106. Gruss, *Apostles of Denial*, p. 104, cf. pp. 56-66, 76.

107. William J. Schnell, *Jehovah's Witnesses Errors Exposed* (Grand Rapids, MI: Baker, 1975), p. 13.

108. cf. the Russell-White debate of 1908; J.F. Rutherford, *Reconciliation* (WBTS, 1928), pp. 175-76; *The New World*, (WBTS, 1942), pp. 360-61; *Let God Be True*, (WBTS, 1946), pp. 79; 1952, p. 98.

109. Their official history has also been altered; see Gruss, *Apostles of Denial*, op. cit., pp. 19-37.

110. *1975 Yearbook of Jehovah's Witnesses*, op. cit., p. 245.

111. J. F. Rutherford, *Prophecy* (WBTS, 1929), pp. 67-68; *Awake!*, Mar. 22, 1963.

112. See note 114, under Roy Goodrich.

113. For primary documentation consult Martin, op. cit., pp. 19-23; Gruss, *Apostles of Denial*, op. cit., pp. 27, 45, 294-295; Gruss, *Jehovah's Witnesses and Prophetic Speculation*, op. cit., Chapter 6; Hoekema, op. cit., p. 243; Van Baalen, op. cit., p. 259; Gruss, *We Left Jehovah's Witnesses*, op. cit., pp. 7, 65-66, 70, 74-75, 80-81, 83, 111, 118-119, 129; Montague, op. cit.; Hesselgrave, op. cit., p. 183. For problems on the high incidence of mental illness among Jehovah's Witnesses, See Dr. Jerry Bergman, *The Mental Health of Jehovah's Witnesses* (Clayton, CA: Witness, Inc., 1987).

114. William and Joan Cetnar, op. cit., p. 53 (cf. pp. 48-55). The Johannes Greber translation is cited in, e.g., *Make Sure of All Things*, p. 489. Greber was a spirit medium who claimed his translation originated in the spirit world. It translates John 1:1, Hebrews 1:8 and other passages the way the NWT does also. Roy Goodrich, head of the Jehovah's Witness splinter sect Back to the Bible Way, discusses the Society's involvement with psychometry and radionics in his "Demonism and the Watchtower." These are spiritistic forms of medical diagnosis. See John Weldon and Zola Levitt, *Psychic Healing* (Chicago: Moody Press, 1982), pp. 53-65. The last known address of Back to the Bible Way was 517 N.E. Second St., Ft. Lauderdale, FL 33301.

115. Rutherford, *Riches* (WBTS, 1936), p. 316, and *Vindication* (WBTS, 1932), Vol. 3, p. 250.

116. William and Joan Cetnar, op. cit., p. 55.

117. Rutherford, *Preparation*, op. cit., pp. 35-38, 67.

118. *The Watchtower*, Apr. 1, 1972, p. 200; cf. Sept. 1, 1932, p. 263.

119. Much of this information was supplied by Duane Magnani of Witness, Inc., P.O. Box 597, Clayton, CA 94517. For further information and documentation as to the Society's claim to direction and guidance from the spirit world see Witness, Inc.'s tape "Angels of the New Light" and the text *The Heavenly Weatherman* (p. 3). A free catalogue of materials may be requested.

120. Raymond Franz, *Crisis of Conscience*, op. cit., p. 31.

121. *Is This Life All There Is?*, op. cit., p. 99.

APPENDIX

"I haven't read any translation that is as diabolical
and as damnable as the JW so-called translation.
...They (the Society) hate Jesus Christ."

> Dr. Julius Mantey; "Distortions
> of the New Testament"
> Tape "T-2" available from
> Witness, Inc., Clayton, CA
> (See note 119)

Letter dated July 11, 1974
(See note 64, pp. 11-12.)

Watchtower Bible & Tract Society
117 Adams St.
Brooklyn, New York 11201

Dear Sirs:

I have a copy of your letter addressed to CARIS in Santa Ana, California, and I am writing to express my disagreement with statements made in that letter, as well as in quotations you have made from the Dana-Mantey Greek Grammar.

(1) Your statement: "their work allows for the rendering found in the *Kingdom Interlinear Translation of the Greek Scriptures* at John 1:1." There is no statement in our grammar that was ever meant to imply that "a god" was a permissible translation in John 1:1.

A. We had no "rule" to argue in support of the trinity.

B. Neither did we state that we did have such intention. We were simply delineating the facts inherent in Biblical language.

C. Your quotation from p. 148 (3) was in a paragraph under the heading: "*With the Subject in a Copulative sentence.*" Two examples occur there to illustrate that "the article points out the subject in these examples." But we made no statement in this paragraph about the predicate except that, "as it stands the other persons of the trinity may be implied in *theos.*" And isn't that the opposite of what your translation "a god" infers? You quoted me out of context. On pages 139 and 149 (VI) in our grammar we stated: "without the article *theos* signifies divine essence ... *theos en ho logos* emphasizes Christ's participation in the essence of the divine nature." Our interpretation is in agreement with that in the TEV: "What God was, the Word was"; and with that of Barclay: "The nature of the Word was the same as the nature of God", which you quoted in your letter to CARIS.

(2) Since Colwell's and Harner's articles in *JBL [Journal of Biblical Literature]*, especially that of Harner, it is neither scholarly nor reasonable to translate John 1:1 "The Word was a god." Word order has made obsolete and incorrect such a rendering.

(3) Your quotation of Colwell's rule is inadequate because it quotes only a part of his findings. You did not quote this strong assertion: "A predicate nominative which precedes the verb cannot be translated as a indefinite or a 'qualitative' noun solely because of the absence of the article."

(4) Prof. Harner, vol. 92:1 (1973) in *JBL,* has gone beyond Colwell's research and has discovered that anarthrous predicate nouns preceding the verb function primarily to express the nature or character of the subject. He found this true in 53 passages in the Gospel of John and 8 in the Gospel of Mark. Both scholars wrote that when indefiniteness was intended the gospel

writers regularly placed the predicate noun after the verb, and both Colwell and Harner have stated that *theos* in John 1:1 is not indefinite and should not be translated "a god." Watchtower writers appear to be the only ones advocating such a translation now. The evidence appears to be 99% against them.

(5) Your statement in your letter that the sacred text itself should guide one and "not just someone's rule book". We agree with you. But our study proves that Jehovah's Witnesses do the opposite of that whenever the "sacred text" differs with their heretical beliefs. For example the translation of *kolasis* as *cutting off* when punishment is the only meaning cited in the lexicons for it. The mistranslation of *ego eimi* as "I have been" in John 8:58. The addition of "for all time" in Heb. 9:27 when nothing in the Greek New Testament supports it. The attempt to belittle Christ by mistranslating *arche tes ktiseos* "beginning of the creation" when he is magnified as "the creator of all things" (John 1:2) and as "equal with God" (Phil. 2:6) before he humbled himself and lived in a human body here on earth. Your quotation of "The Father is greater than I am" (John 14:28) to prove that Jesus was not equal to God overlooks the fact stated in Phil. 2:6-8, when Jesus said that he was still in his voluntary state of humiliation. That state ended when he ascended to heaven. Why the attempt to deliberately deceive people by mispunctuation by placing a comma after "today" in Luke 23:43 when in the Greek, Latin, German and all English translations except yours, *even in the Greek in your KIT*, the comma occurs after *lego* (I say)—"Today you will be with me in Paradise." Also 2 Cor. 5:8, "to be out of the body and at home with the Lord." These passages teach that the redeemed go immediately to heaven after death, which does not agree with your teachings that death ends all life until the resurrection. Cf. Ps. 23:6 and Heb. 1:10.

The above are only a few examples of Watchtower mistranslations and perversions of God's Word.

In view of the preceding facts, especially because you have been quoting me out of context, I herewith request you not to quote the *Manual Grammar of the Greek New Testament* again, which you have been doing for 24 years. Also that you not quote it or me in any of your publications from this time on.

Also that you publicly and immediately apologize in the Watchtower magazine, since my words had no relevance to the absence of the article before *theos* in John 1:1. And please write to CARIS and state that you misused and misquoted my "rule."

On the page before the *Preface* in the grammar are these words: "All rights reserved—no part of this book may be reproduced in any form without permission in writing from the publisher."

If you have such permission, please send me a photocopy of it.

If you do not heed these requests you will suffer the consequences.

Regretfully yours,

Julius R. Mantey

(Note: A slight grammatical correction was made in this letter.)